Praise for william erickson

"The poems in william erickson's *You Don't Have to Believe in the World* are uncanny and bear a strangeness reminiscent of Zachary Schomburg's early work; simultaneously, the poems are spare and sincere, conjuring the ghost of George Oppen. While reading, one has the sense that each word is filled with care–painstakingly chosen, held, placed. Yet the lines unfold 'light as morning.' Yet the folds are dark with fog. Yet wonder and invention are tucked in, opening like a paper lantern. On the edge of each line the surreal and the corporeal merge. 'The world begins / from the nowhere / of your pupils / and flowers / and flowers.'"
– **Danika Stegeman**, author of *Ablation*

"'I sit outside in the weather / and listen for languages,' william erickson tells us. These poems are the result of that listening. In the poet's body, languages build up, until they emerge dense and potent in structures so quiet, so devastating, so multidimensional that readers reel in slow-mo from one delicious soft shock to another. The speaker's body extends into the landscape, and/ or the landscape furnishes parts of the ongoing, changing body, 'folding into earth / like an unblooming apple.' These poems are hauntings, too; we will want and need to keep returning to them, will carry them with us in mutual inhabitation. 'Ghosts are just bodies / too great to keep / hidden inside.' We are lucky to accompany erickson on his world- and word-making journeys, where '[o]n the lip of the desert / [his] tongues pile up,' and so do ours."
– **Jay Besemer**, author of *Your Tongue as Long as a Tuesday*

You Don't Have to Believe in the World

william
erickson

APRIL GLOAMING

©2024 william erickson
Cover ©2024 GUY

-First Edition

Publisher's Cataloguing-in-Publication Data

erickson, william
  You Don't Have to Believe in the World / written by william erickson
    ISBN: 978-1-953932-27-3

1. Poetry: General 2. Poetry: American - General I. Title
II. Author

Library of Congress Control Number: 2024933697

...we walked
to where it would have wet our feet
had it been water.
– George Oppen

contents

contents

contents

Inventions

I invent a new type of missing.

It is light as morning.
It comes back and back.
It is on my shoulders
like new hours and
things to do.

I wake up to flowers
but they bloomed
for someone else.

Inventions

I invent a love machine.
You type yourself into it
and wait, but nothing happens.
You're on your deathbed.
Everything is white,
the paper,
the keys.

Inventions

I invent a machine
that detects when ghosts
are not present. No one
can use it but me.
I am a ghost.
We all are.
We all are.

Directions

Your hand wanders inches
from the hole in your chest
but your fingers
can't find the way.

You touch
and touch
and nothing.

Funny, how there's so much
to lose inside of your skin.

I peel it away and
everything escapes.

I look out for a moment
and forget the way back.

A New Place

I go to a new place.
Hummingbird bodies
fall stiff from trees
like hopes
there,

spreading on grass,
filling my lungs
with feathers.

A Hole Through You

Of everything
cage-like

I think mostly
of teeth.

I try baking
a cake for
your birthday

from wishes
but wishes
that come
off the weeds,

how they stick

to your gums
to your gums.

O, the stories
I tell where my fingers are
fence slats.

Sub(con)tractor

I lose my footing
at the last minute
and it's into the sky.

Death comes like
having to choose
between colors of
house paint and
picking deciduous.

Death comes
like a walk
the moon does.

On the Clearest Day the Mountain Shows

Some winters
I think of that time we
talked on the phone
while you climbed
to the summit.

It's breaking up, you said,
and it wasn't the signal
like I thought
but the snow,
it's quietly rolling over and
over a sound I could sleep in.

I woke up to the blood in my ears.
I looked for your body
but looking is only this thing
that I do from the windows.

Repetition is a Dance One Does

Sometimes
being still
and being still
are the ghosts
of each other.
I am not the one
with this heart
in my teeth.
I am not
the one just
listening
and listening
to this bird in
my palm
thinking
hearing
it stop
is how
it flies when
it's freed.

Becoming King

I've decided to give up my crown
for some eggshells.
They've been drained and dried
and painted with scenes from Moby Dick.

When I miss my crown
I can look at myself as Ishmael
in soliloquy beneath hanging glints
of phosphorus and become startled
and tiny, or maybe Queequeg
casting runes and
become closed.

It's clear my eggshell selves
are more than I am.

I saw my crown once
in the business district.
It didn't even look at me.

Dad's Bouquet

No one appreciates
the moon anymore, how it
says your name right
before you fall asleep,
how it gives mother
flowers at father's funeral.
No one these days takes time
to plunge their face in the pond.

Birthday Cake

Elaborate arrangements of candles
are what really keep me going,

sometimes,

when the house goes dark
and the dark is your voice

in my throat
like a hand
that knows
just what to take.

The Candle Burns in the Shape
of My Hand Dipped in Wax

It's only been trapped
in the water like this
since the water,

since the painting
I made of you lost
its footing and the
spot on the wall
it took
took the
shape of
what's left
when the
flame in
the room
sighs.

The New Continent

I will be the first
to want to go there
but will not want to
go there first.

You will grab my wrist
and feel what my heart
does without me
and mistake it for love.
We all do.

Our fingers are ten
of the scariest things
on earth. When we
discover they're missing
we'll pretend surprise,
look around like
we didn't hide them,
secretly relieved
we can no longer feel.

Our palms are in on it.
We all are.

When I Met Alice

More of your bones
fell into the canyon. All
the parts of you we made
that night in the desert
at the farewell dinner
are lost.
You promised
never to lose
those parts,
but there they are
in the dust
with my lungs.

Exact Same Ribcage

I have to thank you
for the elevator.
It's a pleasure leaving
each day so weightless.
But not one goes by
I don't forget which
floor is mine
as my fingers do
unpatterned dances
on the keys whose rhythm
sped up sounds just
like your phone number.

I stay there all night.

It becomes too dark
to see my fingers,
so I imagine them
typing the right number.

I imagine the cable's
braided steel makes a case
for the weight of my body.

You answer, *Hello,*
and no one is
there.

Picking Apples

There's a really great orchard
in Poughkeepsie where hearts grow.

We walk the rows hand in hand
small-talking below

the beat beat beating
that bobs the branch tips.

They drip when it rains, go silver
at night, grow silent.

We walk row by row for many, many years
until one day a murder
of crows does what
murders of crows do.

Black feathers. A whole sky.
*This is not the life
I'd imagined,* I tell you,

*this slender line in a waste.
This shadowy red sea.*

This soft heavy rain that slips
down and in and hurts sometimes

and stops sometimes.
Alice, are you hearing me?

To Make Acquaintance

I jump in the ravine
behind your house one evening,

folding into earth
like an unblooming apple.

Like a star in the morning
how it finally succumbs

to the pressure
of my eyes holding

everything in them
at once.

Such friends I used to have.
Such longing and such friends.

Inventions

I invent a machine
that grows flowers
for funerals.

You flip the switch.
No one survives.

You try flipping it back,
but it's stuck, bloom
after bloom, a god
rippling through a cosmos.

It's how we all started
praying to you.

Inventions

I invent how slowly
the boat at sea sinks.

I make money
selling chances
of escape, but the chances
flood the deck,
fill up the hull.

The boat sets sail
with no one on board,
sets sail like it were
the last way out in
a long, long line
of ways out.

Inventions

I invent a way to hold hands
with everybody you love all at once.

The pressure's too much.

When it's on, you're crushed
endlessly in a tragic laughing
accident.

Dear Cut-Glass,

It's been longer
than I thought
this trail of blood
would go, but
the mountain is
so much smaller
at its peak than
when we drew
those pictures
into the dust
on your windshield.
Do you still have it,
the baby we made
from all those
leftover dinner
conversations?
Remember, we
named it Alice and
called your parents
with the news, but
no one answered.
The sky is falling
is a thing we'd say
when it was the only
thing that wasn't.

How in the thick
of it we've gotten,
how frightened awake
by our own restarting pulses.
But isn't this the way
we're told to grow,
by holding ever so softly
to the last of our
parts going quiet?

Genuine Friend

I wake up on a planet with no sun.
The days slip from a spent red core.

There is so much rust
I worry I'm bleeding to death.

I feel all over my skin.
I'm covered from head to toe.

Dear, helpless thing,
to whom are you
speaking?

Monocle

No one looks
inside the crying
person's mouth
to see the baby
in the cold.

Belong Self

Having fingers
guarantees nothing,
I found out.

I was in a cave
in Sils im Engadin
when I learned
the black dark open
as a way of closing in.

I pinch the tiny rocks
for hours, until going
backward I become
the first body on a planet
too young for this.

A closed fist is a kind of self-
reflection, a promise of feeling
at least something.

Belong self, I have told you before.

Free The Horse

There is a horse named Free who dives from a three-story ladder at a zoo in St. Cloud once a week. On the way down, his whole life plays before him like an old film, bleary and undone. He forgets his mother and father. Forgets he was born. Forgets how terrifying it is to watch an irreversible thing going backward.

Humility Castle

Many people
at the funeral
decide to play
where does
that bridge go.

They tread
over rivers.

They finger
the rails.

They wave
the saddest
waves of
victory.

An Unkindness is a Company of Ravens

Last time we met
I asked you of the myriad
sorts of unkindnesses

which pecked
fixedly and which
in one fell swooped.

I asked you what
kind of god
it would take

to limber
this sparrow
the basement's been

clutching enough
to feather its song
into earshot.

I asked you to pick
from this bone pile
your wolf made

the pieces for perfect
copies of the children
we were.

What Contains You

You wait at
the window for days
patiently remembering
to live life,
then it happens,
like a dream,
the whole thing
a few difficult seconds.

Ghosts are just bodies
too great to keep
hidden inside.

You don't have
to believe
in the world
for the world
to contain you.

Burning Day

I'm in the chair
in the woods
when the fire starts.

The best I can do
is blow a kiss
from the center

as everything burns
from the middle to
the edges,

a swell of love
swarming the trees,

a sob of real love
to stitch with
the overcast.

I get into that dress
we fell in love in,

but it doesn't work—
it's just a dress.

The problem with things that burn
is they burn from the inside.

Interview

I apply for a job
at the beam factory.
How about your
experience?, they ask.
I beamed over a city,
I say. *Beamed over a*
lake in the hills
above ocean
a beam atop dunes
a beam through the curve
a beam into silence.
I beamed a beam
that became a baby
with arms in the world.
And the last thing I heard
was the door to a room
where the light was closed up.

Pack Animal

I am inclined
to believe the world

has a door through
which I'll return.

I am inclined to believe
the sharp little tips of a day.

Please don't be angry
for what I've forgotten.

There are not enough arms
to keep saving these faces.

Baby Teeth

I sit outside in the weather
and listen for languages.

Not just people's
languages but languages that
aren't languages at all.

Languages that reach
like sped-up tree roots inside,
how they follow what
feeds them until they
exhaust it and how when
they do it's so quiet

like the quiet of the baby
I still somehow contain.

We speak and we
speak and we speak
and I don't even think
we know what the words mean.

Selling Dead Weight

Once in the trees
with my love
I saw the sun
stop for a moment
over the still
middle of the water.
It was closer
than anyone
guessed.
Imagine right now
the light of all eyes
unsealing a day.
See how light
what's thrown must be.
How does one measure
that suffering?
Oh, how I'd love
if my cuts were great valleys
the little blue clouds could bump in.

Halloween

This hole in my chest
is filled with dove's feathers.
For the party last year
I took all of them out
and glued them to my arms
to make wings.
When we met,
the hole in your chest
had a glass pane painted
with mountains.

I asked if you'd done it yourself.
I joked about flying a message there.
Later we lay in the leaves
watching the clouds set a sky.

Some of my feathers
still stuck to my arms
but your window
was replaced by a hole
filled with insides.
I was just some person, I thought,
with a hole in my chest
and not enough bird parts.
How is it we stand
beneath clouds
and still feel
so naked?

Looking For Work

My first day on the job
at the beam factory
was disastrous.
Nothing I made
would hold up.
Nothing I beamed
belonged above
in the world.

No beams above
waves on the ocean.
No beams above cities.
No beams you could
count in your sleep.
So I quit.

It's the first thing
to do when you love
so much that it
crumples around you.

The second's a sky
cut from paper
to hang.

Holiday

The lake
by your house
in this memory
makes a beautiful
way to abandon
the world.

It's all I
ever want
to feel in
historical acts,
how the last
light pricks
the black pools
of both eyes.

We have finally
let go the balloon, Alice,
but the stars, you see,
they're sewing needles.

Unicycle

I pulled our drowning bodies
at the last second from the lake
with the arms of my father's
old army coats.
That night next to the fire
the hummingbird asked
if every night's a death.
Dear god
who sits with me?

Black Birds

The lake
I remember
had great great swans.
We'd ride them
to the dark middle
where the day
didn't break
past the surface.
I'd get scared
about putting
my feet in, but
you'd give a little
smirk,
and I'd go.
There, there!
you say from
high high up,
and I'm reaching
like you aren't
just the sun
stuck in clouds.

What Killing Is

I hunted grouse with my father, too young to know what killing was. Their stomachs were always full of gravel when we opened them. It was how they digested, my father said. I'd wonder how they fly with so much weight, then pull the trigger. How you digest says a lot about you, I think. How you hold this stuff inside that isn't ever yours.

It was a hard, hard day

After a very hard day
at our jobs we stood
in the kitchen deciding,
but neither of us could.
*We made some very
good money,* I said.
*And some very good
friends.*

But all we really made
were saddles for miniature
horses that children
would ride on their
birthdays.

They'd ride into
papery sunsets
painted fantastically
by the local eccentric.

They'd ride wearing spurs
how they dug in the hide.

Then we made love
like the love
that we make
is our last leg
to stand on.

Inventions

I invent a significant number
of hummingbird murders,
hang them from the low branches,
hide them in leaves.

I look up, and they fall.
I look down, and
the bones make
no difference.

How you regret is you live
like your hands have seen nothing.

Inventions

I invent taking pictures
of refrigerator notes
and sending them over
the internet to coworkers.

*The last of the milk
is all yours,* for example.

Or *I found your pond
to be oddly swollen.*

Sometimes they politely reply.
But most just do nothing.

And that's when it happens:
we all climb aboard the boat
but the boat is a voice
in a cold spell.

Inventions

I invent how you see
with your eyes as if
this is all your invention.
The world begins
from the nowhere
of your pupils
and flowers
and flowers.

You see me, and I become.
You see the way I'm seeing
how we're pinholes
in a bright spot.

The Deaths That There Are

On Tuesday there is fog
but on Wednesday, no fog.
In the last mile of sky
before space I thought
the ghosts of the recently
dead would collect, as if
against a pane beyond
which the air is all
the ghost there can be.
But what's true is only
that either there's fog
or there's not, and
the very recently dead
are exactly like fog,
how it lifts and descends,
how its beads on the leaves
are too heavy sometimes
for the trees to hold up.
This thing in your fingers
is all yours to touch.
There's a way and
the way is a death, but the death
is this bloom on a stem.

Pistils and Stamens

I left my body
in a pile of leaves,
thinking fall colors
an effigy, a sun.

Red giant. Someone to miss me.

My body and I gravitate
weakly around the secrets
between us.

Constellations
bloom from its ribcage,
pollinate in me.

A Great, Great Funeral

- after Zachary Schomburg

This thing I find
beating beneath leaves
in the woods
is not your heart.
It does not beat for you.
It does not beat the blood
of the body it's in.

It's a different kind of sun
than the sun that I know
the afternoon sun
that I drink while I read
in the park where the trees are
on purpose.

It bleeds in my hand.
It plucks from the light.

Oh how tenderly one must
stitch the bones back
into a dirge!

Cliff Face

These stones, too, are songs.

I learned only to comb
through what's lost.

A face, the door frame.
A fondness, the forgetting.

On the lip of the desert
my tongues pile up.

Whose Deaths There Are

Deep in the grey ocean,
a death.

Giving off bubbles
like frantic sparrows,
a death.

Blooming at the surface,
a wave, a death.

Port side, your tiny boat
a leaf on the skin,
you sink your arm beneath
the water and something
takes it from you,
carries it into a
brand new blackness.

For the first time
you touch your death.
It always starts
at the beginning.

It follows like
names no one said
until suddenly
there is no one else
I've ever known.

Suicide Note

Nothing says broken like erring
on the cliff's side

to see what
its logical end
has in store.

Millions of parts
of your body
that plainly
aren't rain.

Sinking Shooting Sinking

I was at a shooting range
on a boat in the Arctic
thinking: *this*
probably shouldn't work.

In the end, it's always
the ice with the secrets,
how it closes
around its own wounds.

People think that these
bullets do wonders,
that the water isn't just
blood being born.

The Lesser-Known Facts

The thing about hummingbirds
is they'll die before your eyes.

Just die for the fuck of it,

all at once, like a rain
I never saw coming

catching me in the park
with my favorite red shirt
and notebook and soaking me
to hell and back.

Even my bones get wet, even
my ideas about things like
what painting to hang above
the fireplace.

And that's when I know
I've got to let go,
when my bones wash ashore
on this ocean I made
of myself.

All Things At Once

The car on the cliff
in the wild
is abandoned.

Like everything left,
it is left in the future.

No one asks the baby
how much it remembers,
or else no one's memory
is questioned
the minute they're born.

You wonder,
but being an orphan
is as wonted as feeding
the dead to the roots.

Window Seat

I can't see the thing
my I has become.

Chains drag
beneath the bridge.

A hand
in glass.

An eye inside
the tunnel.

Picture everything
you love.

Picture it again
in hindsight.

Negligent Sky

It's anyone's guess, I suppose,
how it breaks,
how it breaks,

how you look
at the ceiling
and cry
Oh, dear
Alice, it's broken!

Comedy Night

I'll never forget the one about
the notorious cloud of hummingbird.
It came like arrows.
It rained a rain of vengeance.
Its rain ran through
all of the hearts beating
behind ribs. Beating and beating
their entire lives right out of them,
and when it stopped beating
that was it, a ghost.
Do you see now why
I don't think that blood
is what living is?

Automotive School

It takes a brilliant mechanic
to restore a completely smashed bird.
Everything outside has
gotten away from me, like
how the stitches in my gums
are not closing up much.
The dentist says there's nothing
she can do about my inability to
mouth words in a cave,
or a nest,
or at the seance
where I used your name
to fix everything wrong
in the world.

How to make ASMR at work

Cut mirrors all day
and come home with
glass in my pockets.

Suddenly, I know
what it's like to carry
myself in a handful
of pieces,

how all the way home
my body's a promise
of cuts,

a meridian response
from plucking my
self in slivers from
fingertip skin.

There are three parts
to my window.
One: the inside.
One other: the out.

Every Life is a Marriage

A hundred soft wishes
hang suspended outdoors.

Houses built from them
lean windward occasionally,

tempted to lift into wind.

We watch halos bloom
into smoke rings.

We propose with them,

pluck what lights them
gingerly to read by.

To read by your light,
your only small light,

I'll have to turn away
from you.

How The Earth Is

Down on the beach
there's a rock face where
everyone I love
goes to climb.

Winds make a bend
in the trees on its nose.

Sand piles up like the dead.

It is this part of the world
that's quit looking.

I stand at the top night after night
for hundreds and hundreds of years.

I study the sky as it goes.

It goes is the nice way
to say that it's leaving.

Over the Copse

I watch the hail

the way the hail

the way the hail

would want to be
watched

on this porch

in the wood

with cut-paper
parents.

Breathing Exercise

My real lungs are
not inside my ribs.

A hundred tons
of river.

To hover ever-so softly
over everything is everything.

I'll draw a breath

a ghost

a face

a petal
from the rain
to dry.

Alice, O Alice,
my spine has come
loose!

Grass Spear

People just don't see it coming,
the whole breathing
yourself to the end thing.
But then here it is

like the tip
of an archway.

What's through is through
and what's left is the arrow.

I pick it up by the feathers.
I think of the sharp dark
of a beak going closed,

the seeds inside,

how any day now
could just open.

Inventions

I invent digging graves at a lake
at the base of the mountain.

But it's never so much
a grave as a closed-up mouth.

All singing
eventually stills
on the shore.

What we never accept
is we dig from the sand
our own bodies.

Inventions

I invent the last thing
that ever happens.
It happens farther
and farther into the
emptiness of space.
It happens right at
the beginning and
keeps happening
and happening,
like a circle
above my head
I don't deserve.

Acknowledgments

This book owes itself to you, however it came to find you. Thank you for taking it in. There would be no book if there were no Lexi. Though you are missed, you remain. A vast many thank yous also to Mathias Svalina, Jeffrey Morgan, Jay Besemer, D.C. and M. Klien, Luke Wortley, and all the friends who read various iterations of this work. We—the poems and I—are eternally indebted to Christopher Luna and the entire Ghost Town Poetry community for support and for a place to put so many of these poems into the air. Infinite, enthusiastic thanks to Armin Tolentino for friendship and all other things. To my partner Taylor for patience and for allowing the space that poems often demand. To my mom for everything the sun ever touches.

Tremendous gratitude to the readers and editors of the following publications, where a number of these poems first appeared, often as different versions and under different titles: *34th Parallel Magazine, The Adirondack Review, The Banyan Review, The Bear Review, The Biscuit Hill, BlazeVOX21, Blotter, Brave Voices, Buffalo+8, Exacting Clam, GASHER, Heavy Feather Review – Side A, Mulberry Lit, Ocean State Review, The Tusculum Review, Sortes, Visitant Lit, The Wax Paper, Waxing & Waning, West Branch*. Thanks all for doing the lit things.

Especially thank you to Robyn and Lance and everyone at April Gloaming for making this and so many other books such tangible things.

About the Author

william erickson is a living poet. His work appears in *Sixth Finch, Swamp Pink, Afternoon Visitor, Mercurius,* and elsewhere. william is the author of the chapbooks *Sandbox* (Bottlecap Press) and *Monotonies of the Wildlife* (FLP) and the letterpress octavo *Nothing Lied Still in the Sea* (Tilted House), winner of the Netsuke Prize. He lives in Washington with his partner and their two dogs in an old house across the street from a large tree.